CW00569958

This book is dedicated to
Alf Thornhill & Colin Bagley.

You do not get oppos in civvy street
like you do in the forces,

These **two** were the **exception**

Compost ready to use within a month.

Contents

I **regularly** give talks around " the UK, **composting** being the main topic.

I live in the quaint little village of Colley Gate in the West Midlands.

I left Halesowen Boys' School at 15 years old, and within 2 months, I had joined the Royal Navy. I did 12 years in The Mob as a Seaman Gunner, then joined **West Midlands Fire Service**, where I served for 23 years. Luckily, I transferred my pension rights from The Mob to the Fire Service, meaning I retired at 50, with 30 years' service (with a full pension).

So, having 2 jobs from leaving school to retiring; both of which I loved, **I'm now giving back!**

I'm Chairman of Colley Gate Gardening Club; Chairman of Abbey Road Allotments. I have one and a half plots myself, all of which are raised beds and I don't dig.

Worms do my digging - that's why they were invented! I also help to run two trading sheds on our allotment site, on behalf of our gardening club.

A few years ago, I needed a project. Eventually, I managed to get some spare ground from the local council to extend our site. I had £29,000 Lottery funded money and it took me two and a half years to complete.

I created **two full allotments** for people with learning disabilities: one for walking, and one for wheelchair access. Both have a tunnel and raised beds, so **no digging or bending**. Shown above: Peoople from Halas Homes in Halesowen working on their plot at **Abbey Road allotments**.

Worms do my digging, ...that's why they were invented! 🗲🗲

I enjoyed the project but would not do it again for a number of reasons: health and safety, red tape, and the PC Brigade put a stop to that.

I regularly give talks all over the UK, composting being the main one, closely followed by **raised beds** and **no-dig cultivation**.

Trial and error

I use trial and error with everything I do, as I want to get the best out of what I do. I've been composting for many years and I'm still learning.

I've been a member of the **National Vegetable Society** for a few years now, and was Chairman of The West Midlands District Association of the NVS.

I produced quarterly write-ups for **Simply Vegetables** (the Magazine) for several years, I made a DVD on my composting trials through the NVS. and I'm a National Vegetable Society judge.

I've also promoted and talked at a few shows including: **BBC Gardeners World Live, The Edible Garden Show, The Cardiff Spring Show** and **The Malvern Spring & Autumn Shows** on behalf of the NVS.

In addition to the above, I ran Caslon Primary School's gardening club, and even had them exhibiting at the Malvern Show with produce grown at their school allotment. Shown above: Alice and Olivia Simmonds from Caslon Primary School.

There are **2 ways** to **compost:** **" you can use heat,** or **you can** use **worms.**

I've only met a few people who use heat!

When using heat, you don't get any worms because it's too hot - they wouldn't survive. When using heat it's only the middle that cooks, **meaning you have to turn it**. The heat that's generated in the middle kills off most things (not tomato seed)

You also have to **keep it moist for nature to get going**. One no-dig grower on YouTube, a couple of years ago, said he got worms from his hot composting. Hmmm!

> ❝ I have learnt to work alongside nature. ❞ Nature **will win every time**!

Composting using heat

Moving my hand down the metal rod you can feel the heat that's generated, but it's only the middle that's cooking, that's why you have to turn it.
End product: a good mulch or top dressing for any veg, fruit and flowers.

Composting using worms (Vermicomposting)

I need worms in my compost, as **they will do my digging** - once added to my raised-beds later on.

All materials " are **natural.**

My first ever bins

I started off using 4ft square wooden pallets (cheap or free). I had bays for manure, leaf mould and compost.

The bays are straight onto the ground. They are lined with horticultural plastic (any plastic will do but the thicker the better). I cut about 5 holes with my knife into each 4ft square side, so that air will get into the compost. The plastic helps to keep in the moisture and warmth.

I do not turn my compost and never have, the worms turn it.

I started off doing the **layering / lasagne method** with a 1" layer of different materials. This worked well, as you can see when the ingredients underneath have broken down.

All materials are natural, meaning they will all break down, and the good thing about it: **most are free!**

> ## If I can see a worm, I'm happy, 🗲🗲 and so are they!

This was a bin up the back garden, the principles are the same. Carpet lid on top; this drops down as the ingredients break down. I'm lifting up the corner doing a moisture check.

If I can see a worm, I'm happy, and so are they because they are still there. If there weren't any worms, then it would be drying out and they'd have cleared off.

Keep 'em moist and warm and they will eat and multiply rapidly.

" Compost ready within 3 months.

Nitrogen is an excellent activator for your compost. **One form of nitrogen: Urine!**

If I'm on the plot and need a piddle: **the compost gets it!** If I can't reach the compost heap, then the rhubarb gets it!

Rhubarb makes an excellent wine; use the first pickings for best results.

I piddled on the kids when they were young, they're both 6 footers now!

#BostinCompostin

Matt Biggs, BBC Gardeners' World Live 2015. 🗬

Matt was my compere, a brilliant bloke, and would talk to you like a normal gardener! I had the audience in stitches as I told them Matt had kept and donated his urine from the night before.

The good thing about saving your own piddle: If it's clear, then you feel better - if it's cloudy, then it's telling you you need to go and see your quack!

Besides being a good compost activator, it's also a good deterrent against foxes, badgers, cats and the like. I spread it on the edges of my pathways on the plot.

" Making leaf mould.

You usually make leaf mould in a compost bin or a homemade bay. If you don't have room for a bin or bay (you may live in a lighthouse!) Then you can make it from a strong, thick plastic bin bag.

To break down, every leaf has to be wet. No evergreen leaves. **The smaller the leaf, the better for a quicker breakdown process.**

Get a strong bin bag, fill it with leaves, 3 small holes in the bottom of the bag, add activator (if you have it), give the contents a good watering, squash out the air and tie a knot in the bag.

the leaf mould is ready "

Put it somewhere out the way. Mine went at the back of the shed.

After six months, the leaf mould is ready. Add to the compost or use as a mulch or as a top dressing.

Some big boys tell you to make a leaf mould pen out of chicken wire! What a load of... It's going to take moons to break down; the wind will dry the leaves, meaning they won't break down quickly. **Keep 'em moist and warm**, and the bacteria, fungi, worms and nature will break 'em down for you.

🢠🢠 Leaf mould using **compost bins.**

About 20 years ago, the Government gave householders the opportunity to buy these compost bins at a cheap rate, to get them into composting.

Each house was allowed three bins maximum; either the 330 ltrs or the 220 ltrs size. My old man didn't want his, so I ended up with six. I still use 'em all. Two for leaf mould and four for compost.

Making leaf mould using compost bins

The cleaner the leaf, the better. **Churchyards and parks are ideal** as they carry less pollution from passing cars.

The cleaner the leaf: 🙺 - the better

When I get 'em home, I tip 'em out again, then pick 'em up with a leaf vacuum / shredder.

These are now half the size, meaning **they will break down twice as quick** - even better.

44 **All of my bins** are placed in **direct sunlight.**

Add a 2 inch layer in the bin, then water. You can add urine, nettle brew, comfrey brew or liquid manure as an activator. **All at a 10:1 ratio dilution; rain water is best.**

Use all leaves collected or until the bin is full. With my wooden pallet heaps, I had carpet on top. The carpet lid dropped as the ingredients broke down, so I'm also trying carpet lids on these.

It works because there is no cold void from the surface to the lid. I now have activity on the surface. The carpet lid is back on. I do a moisture check every 3 weeks. It's hard to over-water as you have the drainage.

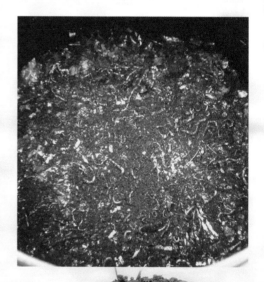

Beautiful brew!
You could 🙶 swim in it.

If you don't have a leaf vacuum/shredder then put 'em on the lawn and go over 'em with the lawn mower. Or chop 'em up in a bucket. **The smaller the leaf, the quicker the breakdown.**

End product from your bin, three to four months if looked after! If you want it to break down even more, then leave it in longer but **don't let it dry out.** I keep this and use it as one of my compost ingredients. It can also be used as a top dressing or as a mulch, or forked-in if you have poor soil!

Shown above: Leaf mould after 12 months. **Beautiful stuff.** You could swim in it!

Compost **using worms**
💬 {Vermicomposting}

Through trial and error over the years, I can now get quick, ready-made compost to use as a top dressing for my raised beds. Still being full of worms; I spread out the compost, water it, and cover it with a weed suppressant.

The worms now do my digging; that's why they were invented, use 'em. The raised bed is ready to use again within two weeks. My finished compost can also be used as a growing medium (neat), instead of buying multi-purpose compost.

My routine; Composting day Monday (if it's piddling down, then Tuesday). The week before: I have been collecting kitchen scraps, but nothing cooked (if it's cooked, eat it.) Save your egg shells too. Kitchen scraps are part of my **overall green waste**.

You can **rip up** these, **while** 🙶 **watching the box**!

This is me ripping up egg boxes **for the carbon**, one of my brown waste products. (Nothing coloured or glossy, just in case)

If you can't do two things at once, turn the telly off! Remember, the smaller the ingredient, the quicker the breakdown process.

In the kitchen, I'm also saving used tea bags. Dry 'em out, it makes 'em easier to handle later on.

One day, tea bags will be made plastic-free!

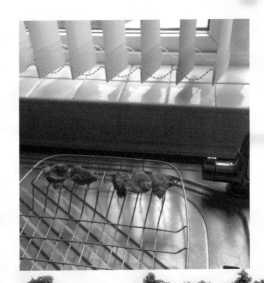

❝ No colour or glossy paper.

The old man went into hospital to have his ticker done. On visiting, he said "Goo an' empty this our kid." I thought: "I ain't throwin' that away," ...so I trod on it and shoved it down my underpants to smuggle it out

Papier-mâché is another brown waste product which is **full of carbon**, so ideal to be ripped up.

I need more carbon (brown waste). So shred the newspaper - once again, no colour or glossy paper, just in case!

> The wine is used to **exibit**, as **bribes** and **thank-yous**

Through trial and error using different papers' materials I ended up here, at a charity shop.

I now bribe 'em with homemade wine made from produce from the plot and a donation to the charity.

I also exhibit the wine at Colley Gate Gardening Club's annual open show. We don't drink the wine! It's used to exhibit, as bribes or as thank-yous.

The **older the book:** “ the better.

I ask the charity shops to save me their paperback books. The older the book: the better. Darker-edged books are what they look for.

If you can get paperbacks with shillings and pence on: **perfect**. The pages smell old, meaning it's already started to break down! Mmmmmm.

The **smaller** the cut: **"** the **better**.

Any paper shredder will do ...I now use a micro-cross shredder. The smaller the cut, the better.

The dried tea bags are opened up and emptied onto the shredded paper. I discard the bags.

Kitchen and loo rolls are also cut open and put through the shredder.

" I give **talks** all over the UK.

This is me on the plot, Monday morning. As I don't dig anymore, **the hardest I work is chopping up my kitchen and garden waste,** which usually takes around 5 minutes.

I give talks all over the UK, I once finished a talk on composting, then, during the Q&A, someone said it was 'too much like hard work'.

God knows what he did for a living if *that's* hard work!

Once again, **the smaller the ingredients: the quicker the breakdown!** The bread bags of kitchen waste are from an old folks' home where my Mom and Aunt were residents.

Extendable 🙶 shears, equals: less bending

Plot waste

Rhubarb leaves are poisonous **but ideal for your bin**. Potato tops get chopped up as well. If they have blight, bung 'em in the council bin.

Extendable shears equals less bending.

Ask your **local**
66 greengrocer.

If you don't get enough kitchen or garden scraps, then go to your local fruit and veg shop and ask for their scraps, or go round the back and nick 'em out of the skip.

You can also ask friends and neighbours to save you their kitchen scraps.

I also get my crates out of the skip. I use these to store my shallots and gladiolus corms in the garage over winter.

Use ❞ seasonal extras

When chopped-up, the bucket is emptied into an empty compost bag. A double handful of shredded paper goes in. Carry on 'til all of it's used.

Use seasonal extras, ie: chopped comfrey, chopped nettles and grass cuttings. Once done, the bag is up-ended about 6 times, mixing the contents.

66 Keep them **warm** and dry.

This chopped up bag is now placed next to my extra bags of natural ingredients, then covered in carpet to protect them from rain and frost.

The carpet is then lifted, revealing the plastic sheet underneath; this also helps to keep in the warmth and keep them dry.

My bags of extra ingredients are now opened up. They include: spent hops, spent mushroom compost, manure (your worm input), leaf mould, basalt rock dust, wood chip, top soil (bacteria and fungi). I use mole hills, seaweed (shredded), used peat (last year's grow bags), straw, wood burner ash. Plus other ingredients, which we'll cover shortly.

If mole hills are there 🙿 Then it's good soil.

If mole hills are there, then it's good soil! The moles are there because it has worms in it. They have also riddled the soil for you ready to take away. If you see someone collecting mole hills, you can now think 'Mmm...a composter!'

I get **spent mushroom compost** by the tonne for our trading sheds on our allotment. Anything I need, I Google it and get the cheapest, usually a toss-up between Amazon and eBay.

This is then weighed out in 20lt bags ready to sell. When I open a bag up, I rub it out in my hands, opening the lumps up; bostin' stuff. **A good seller at our trading sheds.**

Another **natural** product that ❝ breaks down well.

Wood chip ↑

Wood chip is another natural product that breaks down well. Any large bits, I bung 'em out on the pathway. We had a delivery of woodchip on our site. It rained overnight and the next day it was steaming / cooking, meaning it has already started to break down. **Another natural product,** so this is now another addition to my bins.

Spent hops →

You can get this free from a brewery, they need to get rid of it - **get in there!** Google breweries near to your town, It's surprising how many small independent breweries there are around the UK.

Naturally occurring vitamin ,, and minerals

Layers chicken pellets ↑
Spent mushroom compost →
Alfalfa pellets ↓

These are **rich in calcium** and other naturally occurring vitamins and minerals.

66 This is a **strong** manure.

Chicken manure ↑

Be careful, this is a strong manure, so I dry and
shred it. It's then easier to use and not so strong.

Wheat grain →

Wheat grain can also be collected from a brewery.

Use this 🙷 muck **fresh**, straight away

Alpaca and Llama muck ↑

(shown above) Not too strong and can be used fresh immediately.

Sawdust and wood shavings →

Sawdust and wood shavings from clean, untreated timber.

Seaweed contains " **good** salts.

Whilst still sober on my **Portsmouth HMS Tartar reunion**, I collected 3 bags of seaweed, but was told by a man in a hi-vis jacket to put it back. I waited 'til he clocked off at 4:30, then collected it!

I've since found out that the salts from the seaweed are good salts, no need to wash it off! **Surprising how quick the seaweed dries out.**

Once dry
I chop up "
the seaweed.

Once dry, **I chop up the seaweed.**

If it's still too large, I shred it a couple of times.

66 That's better!

You can now use a handful instead of a dollop!

If, like me, you live in the Midlands and can't get hold of any seaweed, **then cheat! Use sea kelp** - crush a couple of tablets.

This is the end result, **before it goes into the bin**.
You could eat it now, it's that good!

As with **all of** my **leaf mould bins,** **"** **these** are also placed in **direct** sunlight.

Empty a 4" layer into your bin, then water it. Do the same again 'til you have emptied the bag.

Add a carpet lid and water that as well. then add the bin lid.

Carry out a **weekly "** moisture check

Once full, put the date on the lid. **The compost should be ready within two months.** Carry out a weekly moisture check.

I need it to break down quicker, **as I need the compost ready**; so I add extra worms.

The more worms there are, the quicker the breakdown process.

“ Ask your **local** groundskeeper.

You can get them from a fishing tackle shop for about £4 a tub.

If you don't want to pay, then go to a bowling green or cricket pitch, and ask the groundsman where he puts the grass cuttings. Look underneath, in the warm moist cuttings, and pick out your worms.

A few fishermen do this! Right hand side of photo, no snow on the grass cuttings!

Put your extra **worms** in. 🥯

Put your extra worms in, it works.

When lifting my lid during a moisture check, I noticed that there no worms!

What eats **worms**?
❝ ...Moles!

This chap had got in from underneath and eaten all me worms, ...then legged it!

My mole deterrent:

Chicken wire is placed underneath the bin.

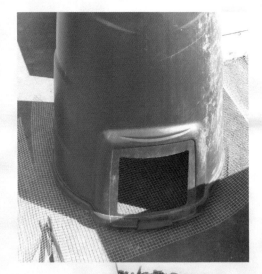

> ## But I was still losing worms!

A few were dropping through the chicken wire, he was just lying on his back with his mouth open! You can see the mole-run under the chicken wire.

So now, when I start a new bin, **I add a foot of straw first**. By the time the straw has broken down, my compost is ready and out! Worms saved!

" Another moisture check.

Another moisture check, and **worms fell out from around the rim of the lid.**

First thing I did was to pick up the worms and put them in the next bin!

Keep **" **
the pH
neutral.

Why are the worms trying to get out? I never needed to add lime before to keep the pH neutral, got away with it by using **crushed egg shells** which provide calcium - this is my lime content.

If you remember, before I got my extra veg scraps from a fruit & veg shop, I had 'em from a rest home where my mom and aunt were living.

66 Worms **love Moist**, **dark, aerobic** places.

It was the ingredients they were giving to the residents (for their vitamins) that the worms didn't like.

Since I've kept out the citrus, I've had no problems at all. If you are happy to add them to your bins / heaps then carry on. But for me, there are enough other natural ingredients to add to your bin.

Remember:

Worms love moist, dark, aerobic (Air) conditions.

I cover my bins 🗨 in **white** emulsion

I want compost all year round; so **in the summer, I protect them from the heat.**

White repels the sun, so I cover my compost bins in white emulsion.

A roll of white plastic 'fell off the back of a wagon', **...perfect.**

" I **cover** my bins with old carpet.

In the winter, **I don't want any worms to get cold and clear off**, so I cover my bins with old carpet, thick blankets, or similar if no carpet is available.

Also, as a bonus: I cover that in black plastic. **This absorbs the heat!** This also helps to keep the carpet covers dry, holding in the heat.

You'll need 🙶 **different** sized carpet covers.

Because these bins taper, you need different sized carpet covers. Place a large carpet on the bottom and replace it with a smaller one, as the bin fills up.

During high winds and rain, a piece of carpet had blown up against one of my bins from the next plot. I threw it in my bin and thought I will throw that away next time I'm down the plot.

❝ Moist & warm
The **ideal** breeding ground.

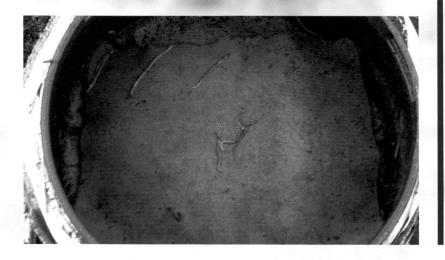

This is when I lifted off the lid to throw that carpet away, because the carpet had gone in wet.

When I lifted it out, it turned out to be an **ideal breeding ground** in between the two layers of carpet - moist and warm!

Because you have covered the vent / door on the front of the bin, you need extra air to get in. So I take off the brick and lift the lid so that it's **unven, not sealed.**

No more paying " for **worms**!

So now I use **three layers of top carpet** and they all have to be kept moist! To get **this many worms**, you **have to** have the right conditions!

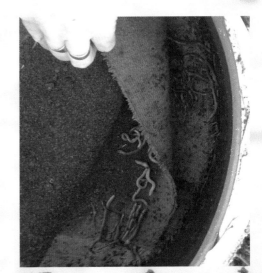

🙶 Use it as a growing medium.

This is the recycled compost our local Council sells at the tip! When I was chairman of Dudley Horticultural Advisory Council, we (the committee) had a trip around the green recycling depot near Wolverhampton.

When the coach had finished the tour around the site, the depot employee who was on the mic asked if there were any questions, I asked **"How can you get away with calling it compost? It's not compost."**

When I got home, I wrote to the letters page in our local evening newspaper the Express & Star:

"As I'm Chairman of Dudley Horticultural Advisory Council, I'm advising people not to buy the recycled compost the council are selling at the tip, **it is not compost."**

A week went by, then I started to get letters from Bromsgrove residents saying "Good on ya." Their council had **that many** complaints, they made them remove the word 'compost' and replace it with 'mulch'. Bromsgrove is our next borough!

If you make good compost, like I do, then you can **use it as a growing medium**.

The plants above are mine, on show to the public whilst I was doing a composting demo at Malvern. Using my home-made compost 100%. I can get nice thick white roots that tells me it's good. **But I needed it in writing!**

This **book** 🟦🟦
is an **upgrade**
from the DVD.

The National Vegetable Society were *that* impressed with my composting methods, they made a DVD on it. **My First mucky film.** This book is an updated, improved edition of the DVD.

I needed to get my compost analysed, so I used this place (above). I rang 'em up and asked if the lab technicians would watch my DVD that I was sending to them, along with my compost sample.

They would then see which ingredients I was using. Once they had analysed my compost, I then needed them to tell me what to add or take out, to make the best possible compost.

" This was the main part from my results.

Comments and Recommendations

>isture content is slightly above the optimal range. Waterlogging can promote the growth of undesirable :roorganisms.

Organism Biomass

:cterial activity: Bacterial activity is excellent. The bacterial biomass will continue to increase and play an portant role in decomposition.

ngal activity is excellent. Fungal biomass should continue to increase.

ngal biomass is exceptional. Fungi will help break down the more complex carbon sources in the compost :h as cellulose and lignin.

Organism Ratios

ratios are suitable for compost. This compost appears to be fungally dominated as the active fungal active bacteria ratio is above 1. Most soils we analyse have poor fungal levels so addition of a fungal minated compost is generally advised. From a microbial perspective, this compost is excellent.

▮ Blue bars indicate that a value is within the optimal range

▮ Yellow bars indicate that a value is above the expected range

▮ Red bars or no bars indicate that values are lower than expected

...Concluding;

"This compost is excellent"

If I can do it, so can local councils and the Government. The Government has been looking for an alternative to peat for a few years now. **I have it. Still no reply from them!**

Most of my ingredients are **natural and free!**

Even now, I'm still trial and erroring. I do it with everything I do! I trialled three week-old compost a couple of years ago, I took the worms out first.

I started off with two leek seedlings; one grown in **the best compost you can get**, the other in **my home-made compost**.

(Shown above): Both trial leeks, on par with each other. Mine is on the right.

My thinking was: after 3 weeks my compost still has lumps in it, meaning this will hold moisture, warmth and oxygen for longer than the best compost! It did.

I upended the leek using the best compost, nice enough roots coming through.

66 A thicker whiter root.

I then upended mine, **A thicker, whiter root structure tells me it's doing good**. No lumps in the other compost to hang onto anything! so water and feed drain straight out.

If we go back to the beginning, i.e. **hot composting!**

A mate of mine hot composts and he has exactly the same problem as I do. When he spreads his compost on his beds, he also has tomato seedlings spurting! Nothing kills off tomato seeds, **no hassle for me**, I just pull 'em out when I see 'em, then compost them.

Compost tea: 🙶 one of **the best** organic feeds around.

During another trial I did in 2019:

As I made my leaf mould, I added a layer of shredded leaves, then a sprinkling of topsoil, then a thin layer of well-rotted manure. This is the end result above.

If you make good compost, get more from it by making compost tea, it's one of the best organic feeds around.

The UK is **years** behind other countries.

This photo is **how they make compost tea in the States!** They are getting farmers to use compost tea on their crops instead of chemicals and fertilisers; and it works. We need to work **with nature!**

Over 20,000 tonnes of compost is produced each year at Laverstoke Park farm. Most is spread on the compost for use in compost tea.

Interest in compost tea continues to increase in the UK sold on the idea, others are perhaps more sceptical. An

66 Compost teas & mycorrhizal fungi.

I make good compost, so I make my own compost tea from it.

I went to the first compost tea seminar in the UK, which was in 2014. The Soil Association organised it and it was held on a farm near Stonehenge. The man standing on the right was the farm manager, who had been trialling compost tea on their land for a couple of years.

The seminars were to try to get our farmers to use compost teas instead of fertilisers and insecticides. Also in attendance were representatives from **Symbio**, who are also into compost teas and mycorrhizal fungi. **I use mycorrhizal fungi on most things** and get it from Symbio. After this talk, I also went to the next four compost tea seminars.

Compost tea can be used on **any** crop. ”

We were asked to bring in compost and soil samples, which we then looked at under the microscope.

The goodies found in my sample (which is being inspected above) impressed all.

After dinner, we had a practical demonstration on using compost tea on one of their fields. The good thing about compost tea, is **it can be used on any crop.**

This was another new interest for me in the world of gardening. More importantly, **working more with nature.**

Always up for **" a challenge.**

The Great British Village Show Information Sheet

THE GREAT BRITISH VILLAGE SHOW - CENTRAL REGIONAL HEAT
CALKE ABBEY
SUNDAY 27TH AUGUST 2006

Thanks for coming along today to the very first Great British Village Show at Calke Abbey – we really hope you enjoy the day!

- Between 09.00am – 11.15am, the marquees will all be closed for judging

In 2006, I was asked to enter a heavy leek in a show. This was shown on Sunday evenings on BBC1, Alan Titchmarsh being the compere of The National Village Show. The leek was to be sound (in good condition) and then weighed.

Luckily, I was up for the challenge. I knew a mate who had spare pot leeks of the Wilton strain. He only had four to spare, that'll do me.

To grow these leeks, I used a raised bed in my tunnel in the back garden. The leeks have **a good root structure** prior to being planted out.

It was
full of 🙶
sheep muck!

This was benching the leeks early on the day of the Midlands regional heat, ready for the leeks to be weighed. Another good thing about this event was meeting Dave Goodwin, on the left of the photo above.

He worked with people with learning disabilities who had entered a leek in this show. I was *so impressed with the work he did at the home*, I went up and visited them a few times over the years. **Brilliant bloke**, and we still meet up now, a good mate. Looking at the leeks on the table I thought I would come 3rd!

After the weigh-in, we were interviewed. **This was the second shoot!** During the first shoot, I had a Kwik Save carrier bag in-between my feet!

I was asked if I had been buying from the stalls scattered around the show. **"What have you bought?" "What's in your bag?"** I said I hadn't bought anything yet and opened my bag …it was full of sheep muck! **"CUT!"** was shouted, my bag removed, then filming resumed!

❝ Using a foliar feed alongside a soil feed.

When the leek exhibitors went into the marquee for the results, Alan Titchmarsh announced in reverse order: in 3rd place was Joe Atherton, 2nd place was Peter Glazebrook, 1st place was me, **'Gordon Bennett!'**, I thought.

The 2nd & 3rd placed were expected to win. **I won because I was using a foliar feed alongside a soil feed. And the extra weight was on my leaves, thicker and wider.** The lad on the right of me was Bant from The Home.

Having won the Midland regional heat, I then went along with the other regional winners to the final at Highgrove (Prince Charles' residence). This was the leek I took down there; **good bit of meat on it!**

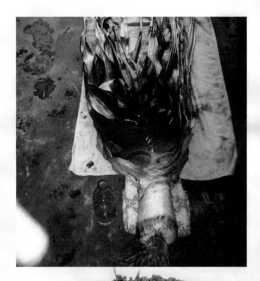

Presentation of **winners** above. 🗲🗲

John Soulsby from Newcastle-upon-Tyne won and I came 2nd. I was chuffed with that. Shown above: Final presentation at Highgrove.

So how did I win the Midlands heat against the big boys?

A month before planting the leeks, because I was looking into my compost as a growing medium, I started to look into the bacteria and fungi side of it.

Luckily, I came across this: EM (Effective Microorganisms). The leeks I was growing had the first use of this culture.

the **microbes** & **fungi** 66 started to **multiply**.

Along with the EM culture and sugars came the brewer.

The mixtures were put into the brewer and switched on; the white pot was suspended in water. Once plugged in, the water heated up and the microbes and fungi started to multiply.

The finished brew was a concentrate and could be stored, with a **10:1 dilution ratio**, soil drench or foliar feed. This is what got me into being a great believer of foliar feeding.

The finished feed was diluted and used as a foliar and drench feed. **It worked.** I proved it with my leeks!

Once I had my results back, **confirming I had good compost;** I then started to make **compost tea** from it.

Compost tea
" ingredients:

To make compost tea you will need:

- One 3 gallon / 15lt brewing bucket,
- 4 mugs of compost,
- Unsulphured Molasses,
  (if using your own compost)
- Air stone with air pump,
- 2 gallons of rainwater,
- Brew bag, if you intend to use it as a foliar feed
  (I use a leg out of a pair of tights).

If you don't have the time to mess about:
Symbio also sell everything to make compost tea, including a compost tea starter pack. Check them out at: symbio.co.uk

Tap water has chlorine in it which would kill off the good bacteria, **rain water is ideal.**

If using tap water, aerate with air stone for 24 hours. Alternatively, use Ecothrive Neutralise from Amazon or eBay. In winter, I use this in my growing cabinet in the loft; as there is no rain water at hand.

Home & Garden

Making compost tea. 🟅

Back to making compost tea:

- Place the air stone in the bin,
- Add 2 gallons of chlorine-free water,
- Add 2 tablespoons full of molasses, (if using your own compost)
- Stir to dissolve the thick molasses,
- Switch air stone on,
- Place lid on the air stone,
- Brew for 24 hours.

The aerobic bacteria feed on the molasses, which multiply, increasing the beneficial bacteria. I also experimented with adding worm casts and liquid fish. (Fish Hydrolysate). A very similar process as with the EM.

" the **compost tea** fertilises & adds **nutrients**.

Try to use it within 2 hours from air stone removal for best results. **A plastic watering can is ideal,** with no reaction, as opposed to a metal one. One cupful per plant, plus a foliar feed (when the sun is off the plants). A monthly feed is good, two week feed would be 'the dogs' (even better!)

Best time to feed is early morning or early evening. The compost tea fertilises (and adds nutrients to) the plants; giving you stronger and healthier plants (working with nature!)

Another product on the market now is **Biosys from Ecothrive**. This is an instant microbe tea for thriving plants (for busy people). This contains a unique blend of beneficial bacteria, fungi, enzymes and plant growth stimulants. Good brew!

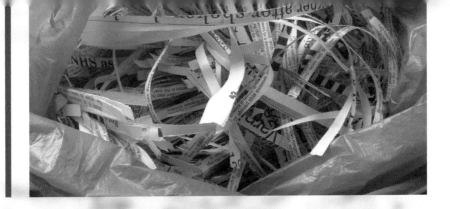

I proved 🙶 **it worked** with my **leeks**!

Visited me mate Dave, in Chesterfield. We always had a trip out somewhere during the afternoon before a night on the ale! This trip out was to a worm farm.

The bedding used was:

- Multi-purpose compost,
- Shredded newspaper,
- Layers chicken pellets.

(Shown above) Shredded non-coloured and non-glossy newspaper.

" Perfect temperature & moisture.

The worm farm use a cement mixer to mix the ingredients.

They ensure the trays are set up in a **controlled environment**. The temperature and moisture are kept perfect for the worms, in order for them to multiply.

The empty compost bags are used to make lids for the trays, keeping in the moisture, with no evaporation.

I've got my own worms! **"**

Once ready, the trays are emptied into the riddler. This separates the worms from the worm casts of which they then sell onto the fishing tackle shops.

The worm casts were being sold at £1 a bag (with beer and fuel money taken out) I then filled the back of the motor up with worm casts.

By the time I got home the next day, because the bags of worm casts have worm eggs in them, they had started to hatch out. **I have got my own worms!**

Would the Better-half let me use the spare bedroom as a worm farm? **No.**

❝ bulk bags of **worm casts**.

The worm farm had *that many worm casts*, they started to bag it up in the original compost bags.

This was on another visit to the worm farm. To get rid of the casts, they were selling the full bags for £2 each. **Good brew!** But a better buy.

That's why I now get a bulk bag of worm casts for our trading sheds at our allotment site. A really good seller.

This is Paul Westwood, he's helping me to transfer our drop-off bag of worm casts into our second trading shed.

Another good way of getting extra worms for your compost bin is to invest in a **10 ltr mini worm farm bin.** They're under £30, and you can grab one from: www.theurbanworm.co.uk

Plus, if you have young kids or grandkids, you can get them involved as well.

The open bucket (above) is me taking my worm bin to my compost bin on the allotment.

Shown here (to the right) is a handful taken out and put on top of the chopped ingredients that I've just added.

" You can **also** add **small feeds**.

This worm bin is small compared to my compost bins; meaning if you can also add small feeds, then it's better for the worms. **This is why I use a kitchen shredder,** which you can get cheaply from Aldi or Lidl.

Alfalfa pellets, egg shells, chicken pellets and oyster shells are now shredded into powder form so it's better for the worms. **The smaller the ingredient, the easier it is for the worms to digest.**

The following is a write-up from Suzie, an expert in vermicomposting;

"Vermicomposting is a composting process whereby (in addition to a healthy host population of various bacteria, microorganisms, fungi mould and macrofauna)

A **select group** of **"** **Earthworms**!

a select group of earthworms that are adept to feeding on the soil surface, are used to process organic matter into a nutrient rich natural soil amendment or fertiliser called vermicompost or vermicast.

Vermicompost retains some unprocessed materials and is used as a bulk soil amendment. **Vermicast is the end-product of the consumption of all raw organic input** and is used as a fertiliser both in its natural state and it's also turned into liquid feeds, extracts or aerated teas.

These liquid fertilisers are **not to be confused with leachate** - the excess liquid and water that may seep through a vermicomposting system, that is solely a result of a lack of absorption and processing by the worms.

Composting worms can generally be found in homemade compost, manure and leaf litter."

If you would like further information, you're more than welcome to join Suzie and her fellow vermicomposters on the Facebook group: **Worm Composting UK.**

That's what you call " a muck heap!

A good activator for your compost heap is **liquid horse manure**. (Above) is me mate Paul Davies on top of *'Heaven!'* That's what you call a muck heap.

They only have two horses, big uns though!

This is me (above) collecting the horse manure run-off, after a good downpour. I have a container full in the tunnel and in the greenhouse. A mugful of the run-off also goes in to a bucket of rainwater **for an extra weekly feed.**

My car is ready to be packed with a supply of well-rotted manure, worms, liquid 'oss muck and straw. **The straw is to top-dress all my raised beds once I've planted out.**

If I want a piddle, I do it in this. "

This is the container I keep in the greenhouse at the top of the garden. If I want a piddle, I do it in this. My next door neighbour has caught me 3 times now! Luckily, she's 80-odd and just laughs. You can't just stop halfway through if you're a bloke! The **Dilution rate needs to be 10 water to 1 piddle.**

Nitrogenis a good activator. But manure is your best one, plus, you get your worms. Three more seasonal greens rich in nitrogen are comfrey, nettles (before they go to seed) and rhubarb leaves.

Pack them into a drum or container for a few weeks, pop the lid on, it's better If you have a hole in the bottom of the container as it will catch the run off. This will be strong, so **dilute to 10:1 ratio.**

Some people soak this mixture in water, if you do this it will stink. By using this method, it will only smell! **To then make your own feed**; pack into a drum for a few weeks (no water required), add a house brick on top to pack it down, and replace the lid.

A tap on the bottom of the drum is ideal, if not, tip up the drum to empty the required amount of liquid. The ideal rate is **10:1 ratio** of feed to water.

❝ Polytunnel, raised beds, the lot.

Not too long ago, I ran Caslon Primary School Gardening Club. **We had the biggest waiting list for after-school clubs**. Gardening should have come onto the school National Curriculum, alongside cooking... it didn't! **I got £5,000 from our local council and did a full allotment on the school grounds.** Tunnel, raised beds, the lot.

We have lost two generations of future gardeners as a result of gardening not being taught in schools. **Gardeners are dying off**, with very few taking over.

Because the kids were *that* hyper, I first got them to collect mole hills, they then came back tired, I could cope with 'em. You can see the school plot in the background of the (above) photo.

I used to put the kids' weekly classes on my Facebook page to help other kids and schools out. One person said I should not put the kids' photos on, so took this for her for the week after! I had permission from The Head, which cleared the school along with permission from all parents, which cleared the kids.

Another good addition
Worms **love** 𝟗𝟗
porridge oats!

Our children **should** be our future gardeners. This is Jacob, (above) one of the kids I grabbed to prick-out and pot-on a young pepper plant. It was then theirs to take home. This was on the **Midlands branch of the National Vegetable Society's stand at the Malvern Spring Show.** I did my bit to get kids involved. Unfortunately I was on my own, so left the NVS altogether.

I once gave a talk in Maer Village Hall in Staffordshire. Josiah Wedgwood (of pottery fame) bought Maer Hall, and in 1807, his family moved in.

Josiah's nephew, Charles Darwin, lived 20 miles away and married Josiah's daughter Emma. It was here in Maer Hall that Charles became interested in the effects of earthworms.

It was a pleasure to have given a talk on composting in the same Village Hall that Charles Darwin frequented.

❝ Looks like I've got the **worm bug**!

You know when you have the worm bug like me when, on my morning paper round for the old 'uns, **I noticed a dried up worm on the footpath...**

Being a good egg, I picked the chap up, I then spat warm saliva onto him and breathed onto him while in my cupped hands. The moisture and warmth brought him round again.

I then placed the chap onto the lush green grass to recover.

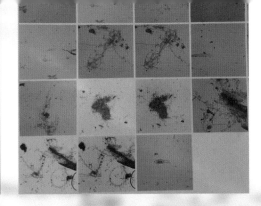
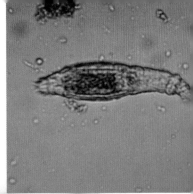

Microscopic animals that eat **organic** debris and bacteria. ,,

A few years back Gareth Hopcroft asked me to send him a sample of my compost, so he could have a look at it under the microscope. (Above) is a copy of what he found in my compost, loads of goodies.

Gareth was taking video and photos of my inhabitants. He then came across something he had never seen in anyone's compost: a rotifer. **He was over the moon**, for himself and me. Found in freshwater or moist soil; rotifers are microscopic animals that eat organic debris and bacteria.

Shown (top-right) is a photograph of a rotifer, taken from the video.

(Shown to the right) is a close-up of an exhibition pot leek. On closer inspection, I saw these little chaps!

Now, are these goodies or baddies?

I sent my photos to Gareth (my compost and soil guru), he came back with: "You Jammy *person*, they are indeed goodies. These are Springtails (soil fleas); arthropods that live on the soil surface. They chew up organic matter into smaller pieces, classed as shredders. If you see these in your soil or compost, then you have a good brew!"

66 Nature **working** away, ...**with no** disturbance.

These are close-ups of the top of my compost bin when the carpet has been removed. If you disturb the springtails they will jump away, hence their name. **If you see springtails anywhere, it's a good sign,** you are encouraging a good soil food web.

Those people that know me will know I love using Mycorrhizal Fungi (a part of nature!) This will be covered more in my next book.

Not digging means you're working **with** nature, not against it.

This photo is proof of what happens when you do not disturb the soil, simply **letting nature take its course** in breaking down any natural material. This is known as **the soil food web.**

You're **after a microbe-rich** 🙶 environment.

So why make your own Compost?

Garden Compost is full of bacteria, fungi and other microorganisms that bring life back into your soil. You're after a microbe-rich environment. I use it as a top dressing on **all my raised beds. The worms then do my digging.** This will also be covered in my next book: '**Raised Beds & No Dig Cultivation,**'

I also use it as a neat growing medium. It's excellent as a top-dressing on my borders around the back garden. Hand-fork out any weeds, stones and pebbles, loosen the soil with the hand-fork. Add my compost, then top dress with woodchip. **A mulch provides your soil with fungi and bacteria.**

Compost **ready** " in **1 month**!

COMPOST READY IN ONE MONTH

MICK POULTNEY

WORLD EARTHWORM DAY 202
SUPER COMPOSTER

Luckily I had an invite by Keiron Derek Brown of **The Earthworm Society of Britain** to be the first of 3 speakers on a virtual meet-up on Zoom.

Keiron also is Biolinks Project Manager at the **Field Studies Council.**

With the theme being **supercomposters**, I did my 15 minutes then Anna De La Vega, founder of 'The Urban Worm' came on, followed by Rhonda Sherman from North Carolina. Rhonda is the author of the Worm Farmers Handbook, plus other publications.

A total of 133 people were in attendance, with feedback being overwhelmingly positive. All talks are on YouTube under **FSC Biodiversity Projects**.

Anyone **can** 🙶 **compost**.

If you have a small garden or small family; it's no problem, you can still compost. I suggest that 2 bins are ideal, 1 for leaf mould, the other for compost.

Use the door on the front of the bin to **extract the finished compost**, it may be compact so a hand-fork will come in handy.

66 Teaming with **microbes!**

This is me in a waiting room, enjoying a good book. This one is called **Teaming with Microbes.**

Here is Colley Gate Gardening Club's annual open show. **One of the largest shows for a gardening club in the West Midlands.**

It's a real busy day, but through the hard work of the committee (Jean, Mike, Jason, Paul, and volunteers) it makes it all worthwhile.

Not a bad show for a small gardening club.

Happy composting

Compost " ready to use within a month.

This book contains no:
- Needlessly big words,
- Waffle,
- Confusing Latin names,
- Bull s***!

...Although I would have liked to have trialled the bull s*!**

Printed in Great Britain
by Amazon